This book belongs to
Olivia

Olivia,

Here are some "Tips and Tricks" for using your activity book:

1. Pages are one-sided, so that you can use markers, colored pencils, crayons, or gel pens. Place a sheet of paper behind the coloring page, if you want to press down hard when you color.

2. Pages can be easily removed for coloring or activity games.

3. If you want to share your personalized book, sit next to someone to color, do the activity games, or read together. For your convenience, we've placed some similar images next to each other.

4. Read these directions and poems with an adult, friend, or older sibling.

5. Your turn, see if you can read some of the words or poems by yourself.

6. Challenge questions: What season is Halloween? Name all of the seasons? What month is Halloween? Name all of the months?

Olivia,
Follow the maze to the
jack-o-lantern.

Nothing on Earth
So Beautiful
As *Olivia's* final haul on
Halloween Night!

THERE WAS A WISE OLD OWL

There was a wise old owl who lived up in a tree.
He sat upon a branch, so all the world he could see.
He looked at a snake He looked at a bee.
He looked at a mouse,
But he WINKED at me!

GOOD NIGHT Olivia!
Good Night Stars
Good Night Air
Good Night Noises
EVERYWHERE!

Olivia,

Use these words:

hat	plaidshirt
bull	wheelbarrow
carrot	pants
pumpkin	cabbage

OCTOBER'S HERE
It's time once more
For cardboard witches
ON OUR DOOR!
Rusty Fischer

Olivia, never to scary to wish you a very
HAPPY HALLOWEEN!

Connect the dots
from 1 to 20.

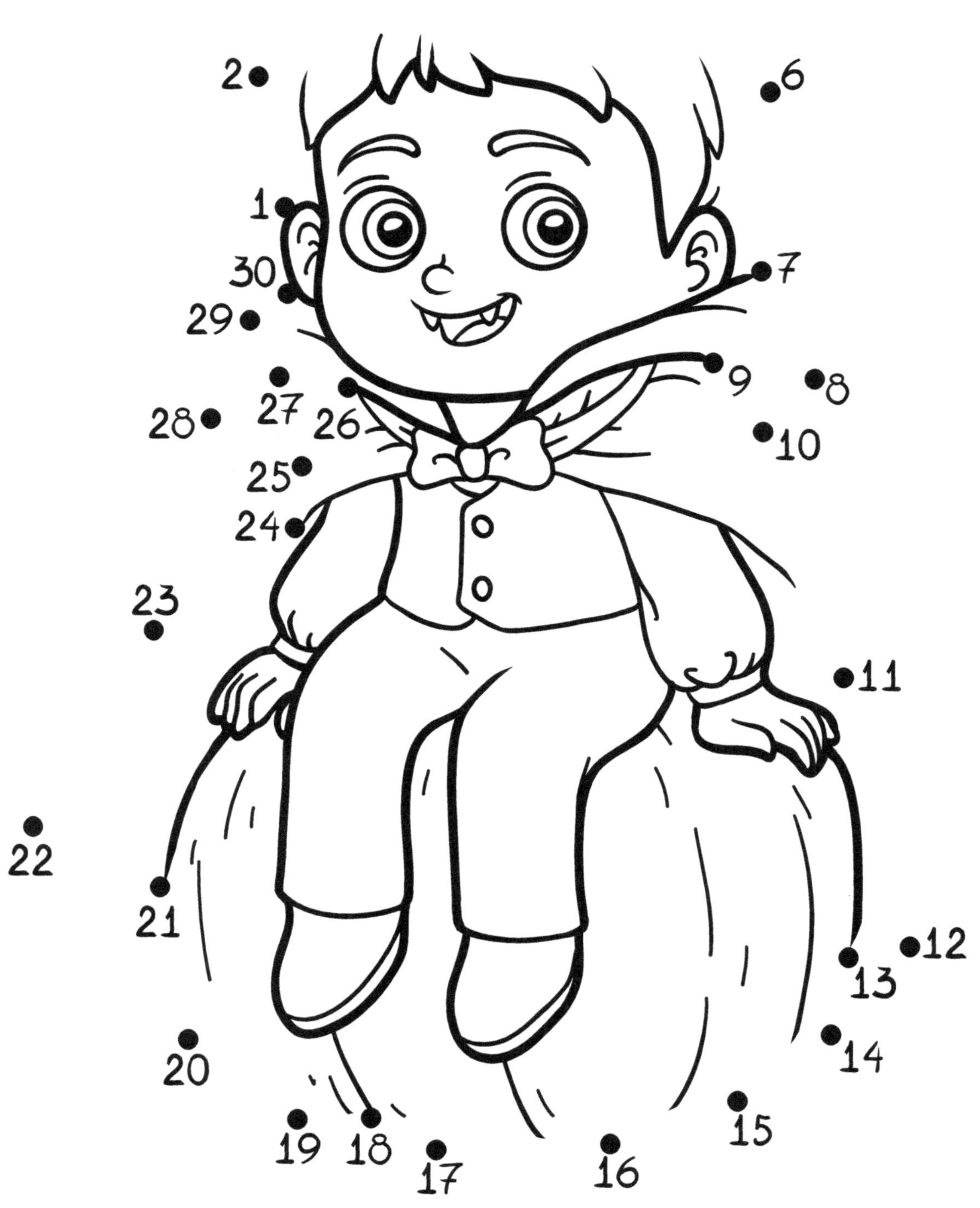

When witches go riding,
and black cats are seen,
the moon laughs and whispers,
'tis near HALLOWEEN!

JACK-O-LANTERNS

I am a pumpkin, big and round
Once upon a time I grew in the ground, but
Now I have a mouth, two eyes, and more.
What are they for, do you suppose?
When I have candle inside shining bright
I'll be a jack-o-lantern on HALLOWEEN NIGHT!

Rusty Fischer

OLIVIA'S HALLOWEEN

Cats prowl, winds howl, witches ride.
Ghosts quiver, children shiver,
Gee, it's keen on HALLOWEEN!

OLIVIA'S HALLOWEEN SPOOKS!

There's a goblin at my window, a monster at my door.
The pumpkin at my table, keeps smiling more and more...

...There's a ghost who haunts my bedroom.
A witch whose face is green.
They used to be my family,
Till they dressed for

HALLOWEEN!

By Sandra Liatros

GHOSTS AND GOBLINS

(Tune of Mary Had a Little Lamb)

Ghosts and goblins,

Cats and bats,

Cats and bats,

Cats and bats,

Witches in their funny hats

It is Halloween!

Olivia's Hungry, Hairy Spider

(Tune of Itsy Bitsy Spider)
It's the biggest spider I have ever seen.
It eats up all my candy every Halloween.
The hungry, hairy spider crawled along the floor
Then it looked me in the eyes and shouted,

"MORE! MORE! MORE!"

Sticky Fingers
Tired Feet;
One last house,
TRICK OR TREAT!
Rusty Fischer

When porches fill
With little feet;
It's time to call out,
"Trick or Treat!"
Rusty Fischer

Olivia,
Connect the dots from
1 to 30.

If you see a witch out walking;
She and her broom must not be talking!
Rusty Fischer

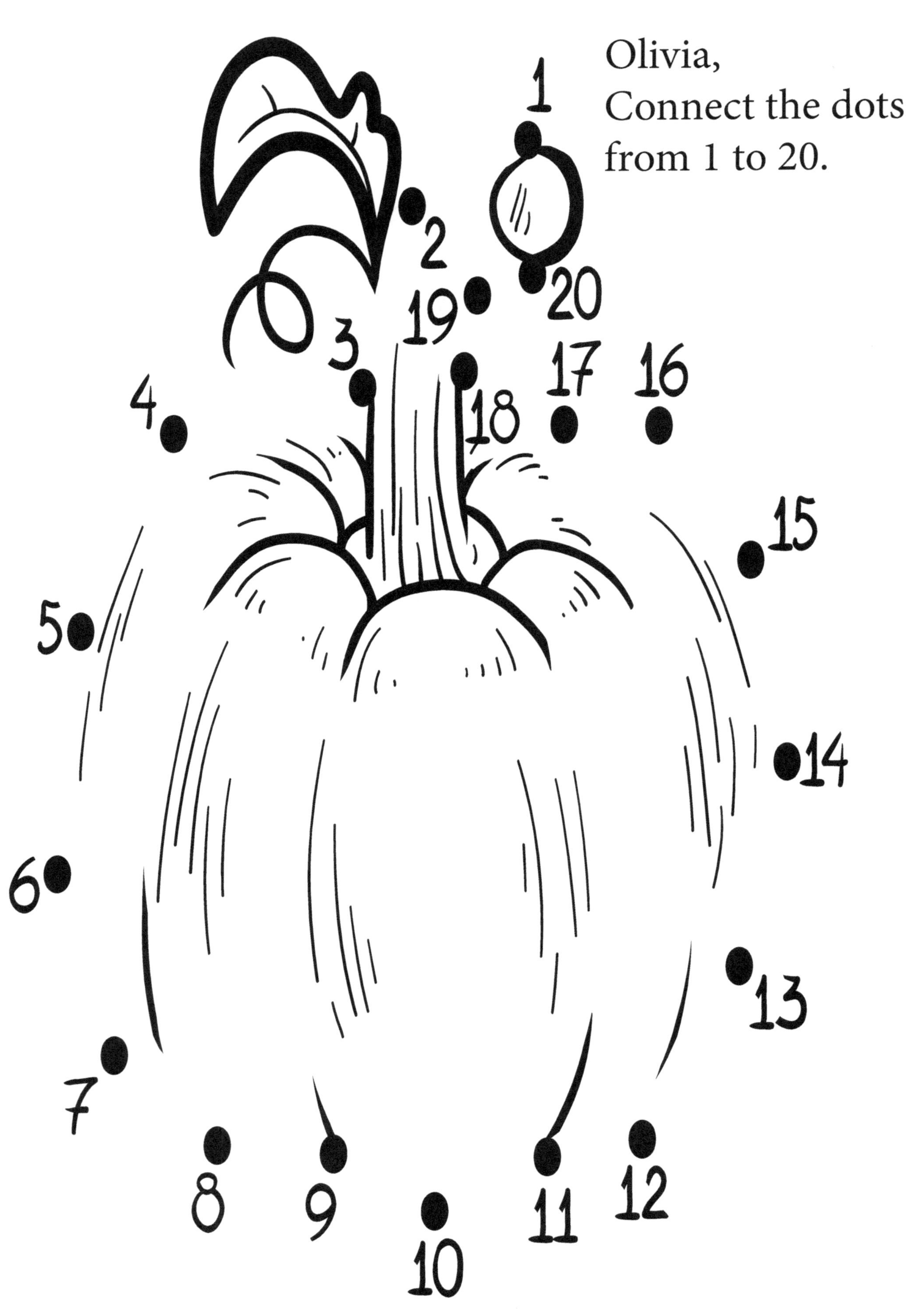

Olivia,
Connect the dots
from 1 to 20.
1
2
3
4
5
6
7
8
9
10
11
12
13
14
15
16
17
18
19
20

Olivia,
Can you help the silly witch
find her cauldron?

ZOOM, ZOOM, BROOM
Zoom, Zoom, Zoom.
We are flying past the moon.
Zoom, Zoom, Zoom.
We are riding on our broom.
Olivia, if you want to take a trip,
Climb aboard the broomstick.
Zoom, Zoom, Zoom.
We are flying past the moon.
10, 9, 8, 7, 6, 5, 4, 3, 2, 1...
BOO!

Little Witch,
It's just not fair;
Waves a wand
To braid her hair!
Rusty Fischer

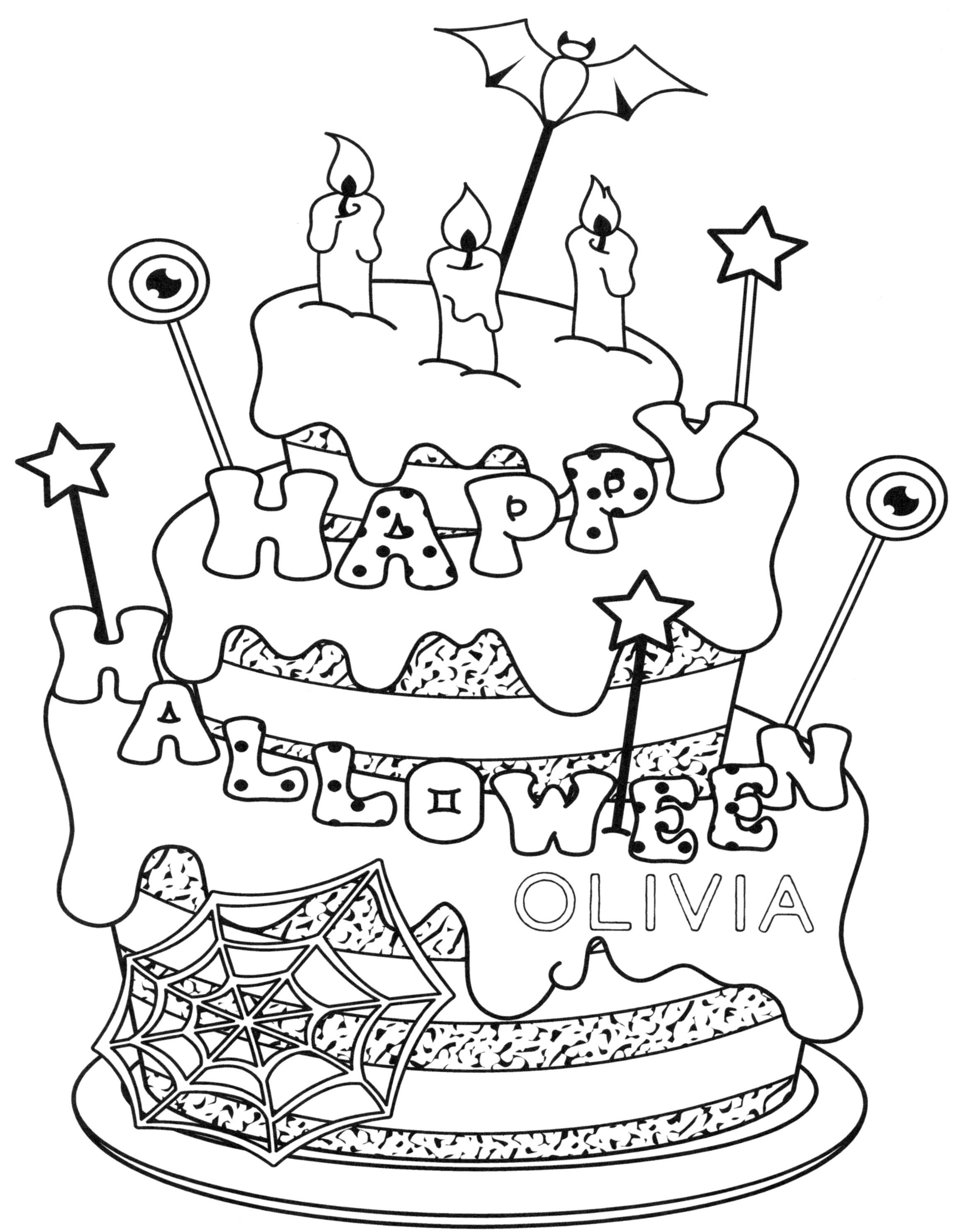

HAPPY
HALLOWEEN
OLIVIA

Olivia's
HALLOWEEN
Party!

Vampire to the left...

...Dracula to the right;
Witches above...
On Halloween Night!
Rusty Fischer

Olivia,
Help the vampire
find the haunted
house!

Watch the sky,
With a frown;
As the vampires
All leave town!
Rusty Fischer

Bat wings flutter
Across the moon;
Remind little vampires
To come home soon!
R. Fischer

There's a *pumpkin* at my window
And a *pirate* at my door!

When *black cats* prowl and *pumpkins* glean.
May luck be OLIVIA'S on Halloween!

Candy bowls empty,
Porches bare;
End of *Halloween*
In the air!

Flying bats, goblins, and ghosts;
The night *OLIVA* loves the most!

THE FLOPPY SCARECROW

The floppy, floppy scarecrow
Guards his fields all day,
He waves his floppy, floppy hands
To scare the crows away!

I'M A LITTLE SCARECROW

I'm a little scarecrow ragged and worn
I wear a hat and shirt that's torn
When the crows come, I wave and shout,
"Away from my garden! Get out!"

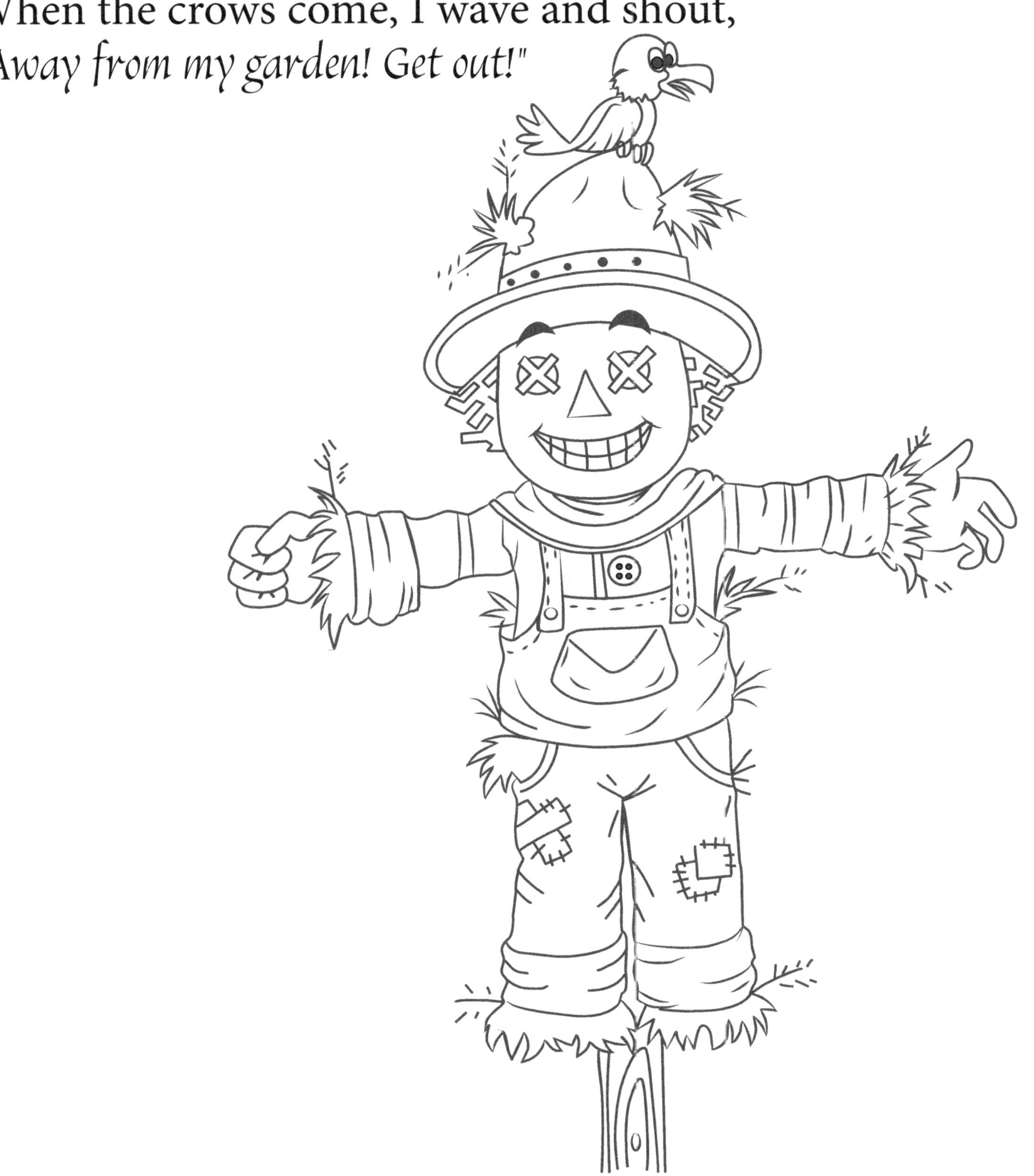

OLIVIA,
We hope you've been enjoying
your coloring, activity,
& poetry book.
Happy Halloween!

By Florabella Publishing, LLC
florabellapublishing.com (Let us know if you have
other names you'd like us to personalize for this book.)